for my husband
Jim

To: Donna & Joseph
From: With love
Mom – 3/16/2001

Copyright © MCMXCVI
by Susan Squellati Florence
Published by the C.R. Gibson Company
Norwalk, Connecticut 06856
Printed in the United States of America
All rights reserved
ISBN 0-8378-8072-6
GB 611

A WEDDING WISH

Written and Illustrated
by
Susan Squellati Florence

The C.R. Gibson Company, Norwalk, CT. 06856

May you stay
in the heart
of love...

where caring
passion
and understanding
become a way
of living
with each other
and with all people.

May you stay
in the heart
of love...

where all things
become possible
and beautiful,
where you can see
the wonder
and hear the music
of the day.

May love call you
to its side
and whisper its message...

that caring deeply for another
enriches your life
and changes the way
you see the world.

This wonderful feeling
of connection
will help you relate
to people ... everywhere.

May love teach you
to speak
the language
of the heart.

Together
you can learn
how important
are those things
that enliven and enrich
each of you.

Together
you can listen
to each others'
dreams.

Together
you can bring
to your lives
an understanding
of your differences

You will know
that you are
each responsible
for your own happiness.

For it is in those
difficult times
when problems arise
that you each have
the greatest opportunity
to grow.

Because
you love each other
you can look
within your heart
and see the hurt
and stay
with the unknowing.

Because
you love each other
you can be
transformed.

Because
you love each other
you will find
new meaning in life
and its mysterious ways.

May all the days
of your lives
be blessed
with the joy
and the truth
of living fully
in the heart of love.

By Susan Squellati Florence

Friendship Is A Special Place
Babies Take Us On A Special Journey
A Book Of Loving Thoughts
Be All That You Are
The Heart of Christmas
A Gift Of Time
Your Journey
With Friends
Hope Is Real
Good Thoughts
A Wedding Wish
When You Lose Someone You Love